A DAY IN THE LIFE
Sharks

WHAT DO GREAT WHITES, HAMMERHEADS,
AND WHALE SHARKS GET UP TO ALL DAY?

NEON SQUID

Contents

Welcome to the world of sharks!

Sharks are my favorite animals! I've been fascinated by them ever since I was a young child. The more I learned about sharks and their cool superpowers, the more they captivated me. Curiosity overshadowed any fear I had of sharks. Now I'm a **marine biologist**—someone who studies marine animals—and I get to work with sharks up close.

There are **more than 500 different species** of shark spread across the world's oceans. They come in all different types of weird shapes, color patterns, and sizes. And new species are being discovered every year! As a shark scientist, I spend some of my time on boats observing these amazing animals. We do this research to learn as much as we can about sharks and to see how humans are affecting them. Many shark species are endangered—the more we know about how we're impacting sharks, the better we can protect them.

My other duty as a shark scientist is to advocate for these **misunderstood animals**. Many people think of sharks as mindless killing machines, but I strongly disagree! Sharks are intelligent creatures, and their underwater world is full of mystery, excitement, and uncertainty. In this book we will travel the world and see a different side of sharks, as we observe what some of them are up to throughout the course of a day.

Carlee Jackson

Shark anatomy

Sharks belong to a group of fish called elasmobranchs, along with rays. Although there are many different species of shark, they share lots of common features. Let's take a look at what makes these underwater predators so good at hunting.

Dorsal fin

The dorsal fin helps keep a shark balanced and upright while swimming.

Caudal fin

The caudal fin, or tail, propels the shark forward. Movement in sharks usually starts at their tail!

Countershading

Some sharks have lighter colors on their stomach and darker colors on their back. This makes it easier to surprise-attack prey from below.

Pectoral fin

Like the wings of an airplane, pectoral fins are used for steering. They help a shark stay balanced in the water.

All sharks are fish, but not all fish are sharks!

Eyes

Sharks have pretty good eyesight. The size and shape of their eyes depends on the species of shark and where it lives.

Nostrils

Sharks have a very keen sense of smell. The two nostrils on a shark's snout help it detect scents in the water.

Teeth

Sharks have an endless supply of sharp teeth, which are organized in rows. Lost front teeth are replaced by the back teeth—kind of like a conveyor belt!

Ampullae of Lorenzini

The snout is covered in small, gel-filled pores, arranged like freckles. Called ampullae of Lorenzini, these pores allow sharks to detect electrical signals given off by prey.

Gills

Sharks breathe through their gills. Water passes through them as sharks swim. Blood vessels in the gills absorb oxygen, which is then transported around the body.

Skeleton

A shark's skeleton is made out of cartilage, the same material your ears and nose are made of. It is softer, lighter, and more flexible than bone. This gives sharks more buoyancy (helps them float) and allows them to move through the water faster.

Open wide

Sharks have been swimming in Earth's oceans for more than 400 million years. These animals have been around longer than trees! A reason sharks were able to survive for so long is their incredible **diversity**. This means that there are lots of different types of sharks living across the world.

Our day begins off the coast of Ireland, where we come face-to-face with a lone **basking shark** as she cruises through the crystal-clear waters.

Basking sharks are very slow swimmers.

Basking sharks are the **second largest species** of fish in the world. They grow as big as a truck! But their favorite food—plankton—are tiny, microscopic sea creatures. Suddenly the basking shark opens her mouth big and wide, creating an enormous net with which she can catch plankton. This is called **filter feeding**. She will keep swimming like this until she's full.

Meanwhile... A nurse sharks finds a cozy napping spot under some coral. She plans to sleep here all day.

Special sensors cover the shark's face.

The great hammerhead is the biggest of the hammerhead species.

Hammerhead vs. stingray

A great hammerhead shark is on the hunt, gracefully swimming through the waters of the Bahamas, a group of islands in the Caribbean. With her tall dorsal fin and sleek, muscular body, she rules these waters. Using her hammer-shaped head, called a **cephalofoil**, the hammerhead scans the ocean floor looking for her favorite prey: stingrays! She moves her head from side to side across the sand in short, quick motions.

Like all shark species, she has special organs called the **ampullae of Lorenzini**, which are spread across her face like black freckles. These help her detect electrical fields in the water—such as those produced by stingrays. She's like a living metal detector!

Nearby, a stingray has buried itself underneath the sand to rest. **PING!** The hammerhead senses it moving in the sand and turns to investigate. As the signal gets stronger, she homes in on her prey. She's found the stingray! The hammerhead goes in for a bite...

Speed demons

Out in the open ocean, there's nothing that can keep up with a shortfin mako. It's the fastest shark in the world! From its large, muscular tail fin to its sharply pointed snout, it's built like a **torpedo** for maximum underwater speed. This is just as well: The fish this shark likes to eat are no slowpokes themselves.

The mako shark begins to pick up speed. Ahead is a school of **bluefin tuna**, some of the fastest fish in the ocean. With several powerful tail swishes the shark gains on the tuna. They're fast, but the mako shark is faster! Before they realize the mako is among them, there's an mighty **CHOMP**. The school has lost one of its pupils!

Race to the mangroves

In the shallow waters off the coast of Bimini in the Bahamas, a young predator is exploring her new world. She is a **lemon shark**, born just a few weeks ago. Young sharks are born already knowing how to be sharks. They don't need any help from their mom. This lemon shark just has one problem: She is still small and needs lots of time to grow!

Lurking in the shallows are **barracudas**, predators much bigger than this newborn shark. She needs to find shelter quickly—before she's next on the menu!

A **mangrove forest** is nearby. Mangroves have long roots that extend into the shallow water like stilts. These roots can protect young lemon sharks from predators that are too big to fit between them. Our little friend swims as fast as she can toward the safety of the mangroves, hoping to outswim the barracudas. Finally she reaches the protective cage created by the mangrove roots. She is safe.

Meanwhile... Trying to get rid of an itchy parasite on her skin, the basking shark leaps out of the water before slamming down hard.

Great white

Probably the most famous of all shark teeth, these triangle-shaped gnashers have serrated edges like a knife. This helps great whites pierce and tear through tough prey like seals.

Tiger shark

Tiger sharks have a wide variety of prey, but nothing beats a tasty sea turtle! The serrated edges and notch in their teeth help tiger sharks grasp and crush hard turtle shells.

Sharks go through thousands of teeth in their lifetime.

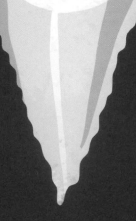

Sand tiger shark

The long, narrow, pointed teeth of the sand tiger shark are perfectly suited for grabbing slippery prey. Squid and fish can be pretty slimy!

Mako shark

This shark has teeth specialized for catching the fastest fish: tuna. The sharp, pointed shape allows them to grab the fish so they can't escape.

Great hammerhead

The slanted triangle-shaped teeth of the great hammerhead are perfect for catching flat, slippery stingrays. Serrated edges help cut through tough skin.

Shark teeth

Sharks are famous for having a mouth full of big, sharp teeth. However, did you know that not all shark teeth are the same? They come in many different shapes and sizes—all specially shaped to help sharks eat their favorite food. Let's take a peek at a few of these pearly whites.

Bull shark

The teeth and jaws of bull sharks are so strong that they can crush bones.

Nurse shark

This tooth is suited to crushing hard-shelled prey like lobsters. The pointed cusps on either side prevent prey from escaping a nurse shark's crushing jaws.

Lemon shark

Like all sharks, lemon sharks have multiple rows of teeth inside their mouth. When they lose a tooth, another replaces it. Their pointed teeth make it easy to grab and swallow fish whole.

South Africa is the only place where great whites are known to breach.

Seal getaway

Off the coast of South Africa is an island packed with seals, and they're starting to get hungry. They slide into the surf before separating into smaller hunting herds. Venturing farther away from the **safety of the island** in search of fish, the seals stick closer together. Their senses hint that danger is nearby.

Roaming the murky waters is a hungry predator, carefully watching the seals from below. It is a great white shark, one of the ocean's **top predators**. A seal falls a bit behind the herd, becoming an easier target for the great white. Attacking from below, the shark launches himself out of the water, snapping at the seal. This is called breaching. **Whoosh!** The seal narrowly escapes the shark's gaping jaws and catches up with its herd. Together the seals swim back to their island home. Foiled, the great white will have to try again later.

Disturbed sleep

A couple of snorkelers float above a coral reef off the coast of Belize in Central America. This reef is a section of the Mesoamerican Barrier Reef, the second largest reef in the world. The snorkelers feel like they're swimming in an aquarium. The reef is teeming with colorful fish, corals, and other marine life. It is also home to a very sleepy predator—a nurse shark. This shark has found a nice, protective reef to take a nap under. She is **nocturnal**, which means she sleeps during the day and is active at night.

Nurse sharks are different from a typical shark. They live on the ocean floor, where they rest for hours. They breathe using a technique called **buccal pumping**, which involves actively sucking water into their mouth to pass over the gills.

The snorkelers spot a tail sticking out from under the reef. They swim closer to get a better look—**surprise**! The shark senses the snorkelers and is startled. She swims off to find a new space to resume her sleep.

Hunting with friends

Lemon sharks are named for their yellowish skin.

As the clock strikes two, the young lemon shark is getting hungry. She decides to leave the safety of her mangrove nursery to hunt for food. No more predators are nearby—**the coast is clear!** She cautiously swims out from the roots into the open water.

During her hunt, she meets more young lemon sharks. They might be her brothers or sisters. These young sharks know that it is better for their survival if they form a group and **hunt together**, rather than try to make it alone. Together, the hungry little sharks swim into seagrass beds searching for their next meal. The largest of the sharks takes the lead in hunting for small fish. They need to eat as fast as possible so they can grow bigger and be able to defend themselves better against predators like barracudas.

Meanwhile... A bonnethead shark has caught some lunch. Yum! One of their favorite foods is squid. Seems like this one hit the squid jackpot!

The walking shark

The afternoon brings low tide in Australia. An epaulette shark has been waiting for this very moment to begin his hunt. Low tides temporarily drain ocean water from the coast, causing **rock pools** to form. These are small pools of water trapped in the rocks. Rock pools are the hunting grounds of epaulette sharks.

A few hours ago, he was underwater swimming among the rocks. Now, the epaulette shark is completely out of water, but he's just fine. He can **survive out of the water** for up to three hours. Instead of swimming, he begins to use his large, flappy fins to walk around the rock pools, searching for his next meal. With his pectoral and pelvic fins, he pushes himself forward and wiggles his body from side to side. The shallow water of the rock pools makes it easier for him to trap and capture prey. There's no way they can escape!

Shark habitats

Sharks have adapted to live in a wide range of different places, from the cold, dark depths of the ocean to warm and shallow tropical waters. You can find sharks in most aquatic habitats around the world. Let's take a peek at a few.

Open ocean

Miles offshore from coastal areas is the open ocean, stretching for miles across the globe. It's called the pelagic zone—a seemingly infinite expanse of blue. Sharks who live here are called pelagic sharks. These sharks are always on the move. They travel thousands of miles with no land in their way.

Coral reefs

Coral reefs are like underwater rainforests. They are the most biodiverse marine habitats in the world! With a wide variety of prey to eat, many shark species call these beautiful underwater structures their home.

Artificial reefs

Shipwrecks, fallen planes, and... cars? Artificial reefs are made of human-made structures like these that have wound up in the ocean. Over time fish, sharks, and other animals move in to artificial reefs and make them their home. They are great places to go snorkeling!

Kelp forests

Tall green and brown seaweed, called kelp, makes up dense underwater forests found in chilly coastal waters. Kelp provides cover for stealthy sharks who are hunting for a meal.

Mangroves

Mangroves are trees that can live in salty water. The tree roots of red mangroves create a habitat for small animals in shallow, warm water. This habitat is important for baby sharks.

Battle of the predators

The great white shark is the ruler of the ocean, scared of no one, right? Wrong! Still frustrated by his inability to catch a seal earlier, our great white is cruising in his hunting grounds off the coast of South Africa. Maybe he'll have better luck finding a meal this afternoon.

Alas, he's not the only **top predator** in the area looking for a tasty seal to eat. Suddenly the shark senses something that fills him with dread. A far off sound, but an unmistakable one—a pod of orcas!

Orcas, also known as **killer whales**, are large, intelligent predators that strategically hunt in groups. They grow much larger than great whites and are even known to attack and eat them! The great white's instincts tell him the area is now dangerous. He changes direction to make a swift exit. Since this area is no longer safe, the great white probably won't return to these hunting grounds for up to a year.

Orcas target great whites for their protein-rich livers.

Hooked

Cruising through the open ocean in the late afternoon, the shortfin mako shark picks up a scent nearby. Her eye catches sight of a fish suspended in the water. She can't pass up this easy meal... **CHOMP!** She takes a bite—but wait! Something is stuck in her mouth, and she's being pulled to the surface.

Bobbing above water on a boat are a group of marine biologists. They're hoping to attach a **satellite tag** to this mako shark so they can track her movement across the ocean. This will teach them about her behavior. The biologists bring the mako alongside their research boat, making sure she is comfortably in the water and **able to breathe**. They quickly take measurements, blood samples, and a small piece of skin from the shark to analyze in the laboratory, back on land. Lastly, the satellite tag is attached to her dorsal fin before she is released. Relieved, she makes a speedy exit.

Scientists use a special circular hook to catch sharks. It's safer for them.

Satellite tags can last for years—and they don't disturb the shark.

Shark babies

In the southwest Atlantic Ocean, a large sand tiger shark slowly swims through murky water. With her mouth in a permanent grin, she reveals rows of sharply pointed teeth. Her stomach is big and round, but not because she is full of food. She is **pregnant** and will give birth to baby sharks, called pups, in a few weeks!

Inside her are two organs called uteruses. And in each of them there is a **deadly battle** taking place between her pups. She began her pregnancy with a dozen pups, but now there are just a handful left in each uterus. The siblings have been **eating one another!** The mother shark's stomach is a cannibalistic battleground for the siblings.

The largest pup in one uterus begins to eat her mother's unfertilized eggs, growing even bigger than her siblings. She needs to grow large enough to fend for herself when she is born. Only the **strongest shark** in the uterus will survive!

Because the sand tiger shark has two uteruses, she will give birth to two live pups.

An unusual shark

Swimming in warm waters off the coast of Florida is the smallest species of hammerhead: a **bonnethead shark**. He quickly moves along the shallow seafloor, wiggling his head from side to side as he scans the sand for crabs or squid.

Having no luck finding dinner on the bottom, he swims toward a **seagrass meadow** to continue his search. There are many small animals living among the seagrass that the bonnethead can munch on. He finds a small crab and takes a bite. Tasty, but he's still hungry—so for his main course, he nibbles on seagrass! Bonnetheads are unlike any other sharks. They are **omnivorous**, which means that they eat both meat and plants. Yummy seagrass is the perfect addition to this bonnethead's dinner!

Shark skin

Shark skin is made of microscopic teeth-like scales called dermal denticles. They make their skin feel like sandpaper! Like sharks themselves, not all denticles are the same. Different species have different shapes that serve cool and unique purposes.

Nurse shark

As you've seen, nurse sharks like to nap underneath coral and rocky reefs. Flat, thick, and tough denticles protect nurse sharks while they swim among these sharp structures.

Tiger shark

Tiger sharks have very pointy dermal denticles. These protect the sharks from the rough, sandy seafloor and prevent pesky parasites from attaching to their skin. They also come in handy against bites from other sharks!

Mako shark

Because mako sharks have to be fast to catch their prey, their dermal denticles are sleek and narrow. This helps the shark slice through the water at high speeds.

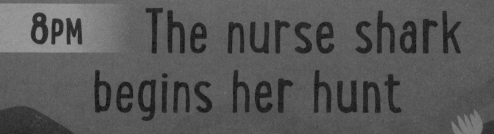

8PM The nurse shark begins her hunt

As the sun begins to set above the ocean, the nurse shark wakes from her (second) reef bed. Although her sleep was disturbed by snorkelers, she still managed to get a decent rest. As the moon rises, the reef becomes quiet. While lots of fish head for safe places to spend the night, the nurse shark's day is just beginning.

She uses her large, winglike **pectoral fins** to push herself out of her resting spot. Slowly, she glides along the seafloor, looking for a meal.

It's dark, and she can't see very well at night. But this nurse shark doesn't need to see with her eyes. Whisker-like **barbels** under her nostrils help her feel beneath the sand, searching for prey that may be buried. She picks up a scent and senses a conch, a type of large sea snail, moving ahead of her. She swims up to it and with a movement of her powerful jaws creates a powerful suction. **SLURP**—she sucks the conch right out of its shell like a vacuum cleaner! Then she uses special teeth designed for crushing shells to eat the remains of the conch, before heading out again over the seafloor.

Dinner under the stars

The ocean reflects a night sky full of shimmering stars and the bright moon. A gentle giant is feeding just beneath the ocean waves, blending in with the brilliant sky. It is a whale shark, the **biggest fish** in the entire ocean.

Growing as big as a school bus, he feeds on the smallest animals in the ocean— plankton. These tiny, microscopic organisms are pushed along the ocean's surface by wind and ocean currents, and they're at the very bottom of the food chain.

Like the basking shark, the whale shark filter feeds—he doesn't have teeth to chew his food. Instead, he swims with his mouth wide open, sucking water over his gills. Plankton are then trapped by filters, which act like a mesh net. Hours will pass by as he feasts under the stars, eating millions and millions of plankton until he feels full.

Plankton

Hiding from danger

As night falls, the tide has returned to the rocky coast of Australia. Ocean water washes into the rock pools, and the area is once again underwater. No longer on dry land, our epaulette shark has switched back from walking to swimming. He makes his way across the rocky reef looking for a place to rest. Spotting a nice-looking nook, he uses his pectoral fins to walk across the sandy bottom to check it out. Walking underwater is much easier than walking on land for him! Suddenly his senses tell him **danger is nearby**, so he tucks himself underneath the first bit of coral he sees. The epaulette is not the biggest predator around these reefs and could easily become someone else's dinner. Sure enough, there's a big fish called a grouper prowling the reef. The epaulette shark squeezes tighter into his shelter, hoping the predator won't notice him. He'll wait there until it is safe to leave.

There are two
high tides and
two low tides
every 24 hours.

Nighttime cookies

The late night brings out some peculiar-looking marine animals. One of those is the small but mighty **cookiecutter shark**. As the moon rises, he emerges from the cold, dark depths of the ocean, making for the surface—his hunting ground. This little shark shows off his big, circular-shaped jaws full of razor-sharp teeth. He's looking for a nice, blubbery animal to take a cookie-cutter bite out of!

The cookiecutter uses the **bioluminescence** on its body to lure prey closer. He has glowing green eyes and a glowing belly.

An **unsuspecting dolphin** swims into the area. Although it's many times larger than the cookiecutter, it's the perfect prey for this shark. The cookiecutter swims close and latches on to the dolphin, sinking his teeth into the thick blubber. Living up to his name, he rolls his body around and carves out a cookie-shaped piece of flesh. He'll hunt a few more times over the course of the night before returning to the deep ocean.

Meanwhile... The sand tiger shark has given birth to two healthy pups. The pups are big and strong after eating all of their siblings while inside their mother. They're now ready to take on the ocean!

Glossary

Ampullae of Lorenzini
Small, jelly-filled pores on a shark's snout that help it sense electrical signals underwater.

Barbels
Whisker-like organs hanging underneath the snouts of some shark species. They help them sense prey.

Bioluminescence
The ability of an animal to make its own light.

Breaching
Jumping out of the water.

Cartilage
A flexible, bone-like material that makes up a shark's skeleton.

Cephalofoil
The name for the hammer-shaped head of all hammerhead shark species.

Dermal denticles
What shark skin is made of. It makes them feel like sandpaper.

Filter feeding
A method of feeding some sharks use, where their gills act like a net to separate tiny food from the water.

Gills
Small slits along the side of a shark's head that help it breathe.

Marine biologist
A person who studies animals that live in the ocean.

Omnivore
Something that eats both meat and plants.

Parasite
A living thing that benefits by living in or on another living thing.

Pelagic zone
Open water areas in the ocean that are not close to land.

Plankton
Microscopic animals that live on the surface of the ocean and are carried along by tides and wind.

Predator
An animal that hunts and eats other animals.

Prey
An animal that is hunted and eaten by another animal.

Pup
A baby shark.

Uterus
An organ inside female sharks where fertilized eggs develop into baby sharks.

Index

This has been a

NEON ⬛ SQUID

production

To the little Black and brown girls like me who are passionate about marine biology, know that you belong in this space and deserve to be here. Follow your dreams and don't let anyone tell you what you can't do. Also, shout-out to my parents for getting me my first shark book, which sparked my passion to study sharks!

Author: Carlee Jackson
Illustrator: Chaaya Prabhat
US Editor: Allison Singer

Neon Squid would like to thank:
Jane Simmonds for proofreading.

Copyright © 2022 St. Martin's Press
120 Broadway, New York, NY 10271

Created for St. Martin's Press
by Neon Squid
The Stables, 4 Crinan Street,
London, N1 9XW

EU representative: Macmillan
Publishers Ireland Ltd,
1st Floor, The Liffey Trust Centre,
117–126 Sheriff Street Upper,
Dublin 1, D01 YC43

10 9 8 7 6 5 4 3 2 1

The right of Carlee Jackson to be identified as the author of this work has been asserted in accordance with the Copyright, Designs and Patents Act, 1988.

Library of Congress Cataloging-in-Publication Data is available.

Printed and bound by Vivar Printing in Malaysia.

ISBN: 978-1-684-49219-0

Published in May 2022.

www.neonsquidbooks.com